My First Book about the Desert Animal Alphabet

Amazing Animal Books Children's Picture Books

By Molly Davidson

Mendon Cottage Books

JD-Biz Publishing

Read More Amazing Animal Books

Purchase at Amazon.com

Download Free Books!
http://MendonCottageBooks.com

 is for an African Porcupine

These porcupines live in the Sahara Desert in Africa, Sicily, and Italy.

They eat insects, but mostly plants and grasses.

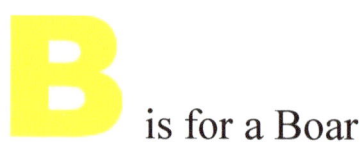 is for a Boar

A baby boar is called a squeaker.

Boars like to live in the desert and eat roots, earthworms, tree bark, lizards, berries, and more.

Adult boars weigh about 110 pounds.

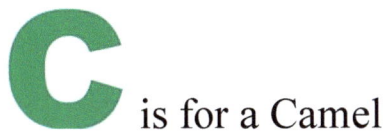

C is for a Camel

A camel's hump stores a fatty tissue, which they can use for energy.

Camels have three layers of eyelids to help protect them from the blowing sand.

D is for a Dassie Rat

NH53 © <u>Wikimedia Commons</u>

Dassie rats live in the deserts of Africa, and are nicknamed the rock rat.

They eat mostly grass, but if they can find it, they like fruit and seeds too.

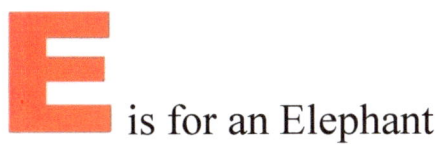 is for an Elephant

Elephants spend 16 hours a day eating and only 4 hours sleeping.

Their trunks have over 40,000 muscles in them!

They can drink up to 20 gallons of water per day.

F

is for a Fennec Fox

Kkonstan © <u>Wikimedia Commons</u>

Fennec foxes have large ears which help keep them cool in the hot desert sun.

They have hairy feet which helps protect their feet from burning on the hot sand.

 is for a Gecko

Geckos have clear eyelids, and they lick them with their tongue to clean them.

Geckos have a special substance on their toes that helps them stick to almost any surface.

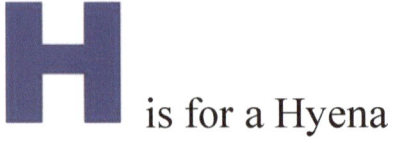 is for a Hyena

Hyenas live in the African desert and are closely related to cats, not dogs.

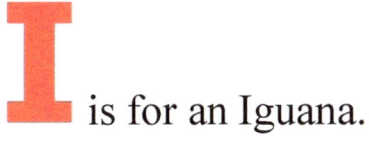 is for an Iguana.

Iguanas are cold blooded, so they have to live in the warm sunny desert, so they can keep themselves warm and alive.

 is for a Jackrabbit

Jackrabbits live in the western and central United States, mostly in desert areas.

The can run as fast as 40 miles per hour (mph).

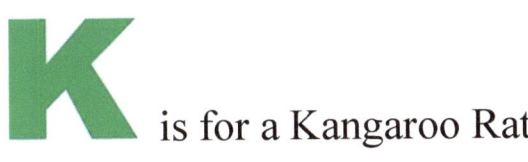 is for a Kangaroo Rat

NPS © <u>Wikimedia Commons</u>

Kangaroo rats in the North American deserts and hop around like a kangaroo, but they are not related.

They can go without water for several days, even longer than a camel.

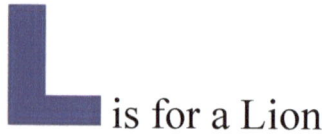 is for a Lion

A lion's roar can be heard up to 5 miles away.

Most loins live in Africa, but a few live in India.

The girls do all the hunting for the group, which is called a pride.

M  is for Mule Deer

Mule deer live many places deserts, forests, and the mountains of the western U.S.

They eat mostly grass, tree, and shrubs.

Boys are called bucks, girls are known as does, and babies are called fawns.

 is for the Nine-Banded Armadillo

The nine-banded armadillo gives birth to four identical babies, every year.

They have really bad eyesight, but can smell really well.

O is for an Owl

Desert owls build their nests in cracks and holes of cliffs.

Owls hunt mostly at night; they eat voles, mice, and large insects.

P is for a Paisano Roadrunner

Roadrunners usually run about 20 piles per hour (mph) but some can run as fast as 26 mph.

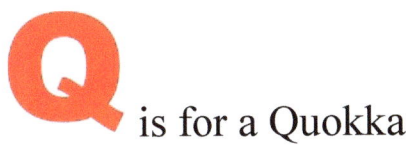 is for a Quokka

A quokka is a type of kangaroo that lives in Australia

It weighs only 6 pounds and it about 3 feet long.

R is for rattlesnake.

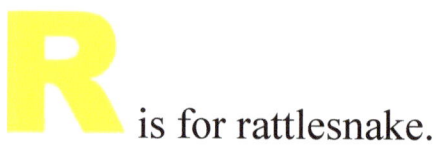

Rattlesnakes can be any length from about 1 to 8 feet.

Humans that are bit by rattlesnakes rarely die; they usually can get medical help fast enough.

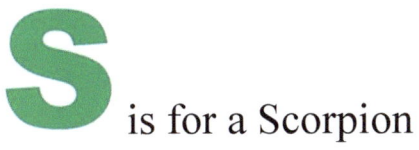

S is for a Scorpion

To kill their prey, scorpions will inject them with venom that paralyzes them so they can eat them.

They have been on the Earth for over 430 million years.

T

is for a Tarantula

Tarantulas kill their prey by crushing it; they don't have very strong venom.

Some tarantulas can live up to 30 years.

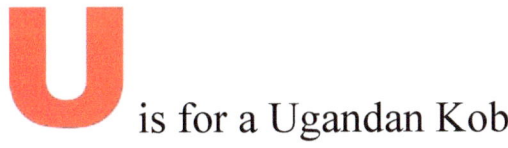 is for a Ugandan Kob

A Ugandan kob is a type of antelope that live in the Saharan Desert.

The Ugandan kob is on the coat of arms of Uganda.

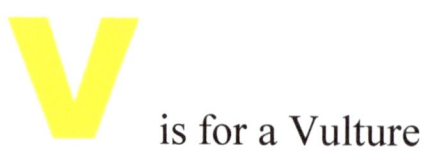 **is for a Vulture**

Vultures can smell a decaying animal up to 5 mile away!

A group of vultures is called a wake, and there can be up to 100 birds eating a kill at the same time.

 is for a Wren

A type of wren is known as the cactus wren, and it live in the southwest U.S. and Mexico.

A cactus wren will peck a hole in a cactus to build its nest.

 is for xenus.

![Xenus]Hans Hillewaert © **Wikimedia Commons**

Xenus are a ground squirrel that lives in South African desert.

They only weigh 1 to 2 pounds.

Y

 is for a Yellow- Headed Caracara

In the summer, yellow-headed caracaras live in the savannas eating ticks off grazing cattle.

They usually live in a large nest shared by many caracara.

Z is for a Zebra

Zebra's only live in Africa.

They are one of the fastest land animals; they can run up to 50 miles per hour (mph).

Every zebra has a different pattern of stripes, no two are the same.

Download Free Books!

http://MendonCottageBooks.com

Our books are available at

1. Amazon.com

2. Barnes and Noble

3. Itunes

4. Kobo

5. Smashwords

6. Google Play Books

Download Free Books!
http://MendonCottageBooks.com

Publisher

JD-Biz Corp

P O Box 374

Mendon, Utah 84325

http://www.jd-biz.com/